W9-CFB-904

If I Were A...
DOCTOR
The medical world in pictures!

NorthParadePublishing

Published in 2011 by North Parade Publishing Ltd.
4 North Parade
Bath
BA1 1LF
UK

All rights reserved

© North Parade Publishing Ltd.

If I Were A...
DOCTOR
The medical world in pictures!

INTRODUCTION

One profession that always intrigues (and sometimes scares) children is that of the doctor.

This book take away the mystery surrounding the medical professional and acquaints children with the person who is so important to their health and well being.

This book is a journey in pictures into the world of the doctor.

An easy read book for children, it acquaints children with the various activities that doctors have to perform throughout their day.

The pictures in the book have been carefully selected for the depth of feeling and emotion that they convey.

Brief text is designed for easy reading by the early reader to compliment the photography.

Doctors takes care of us when we are not well. It is their job to make us feel better. They treat all kinds of illnesses and injuries.

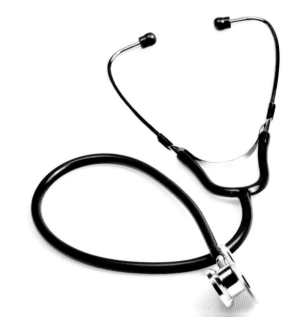

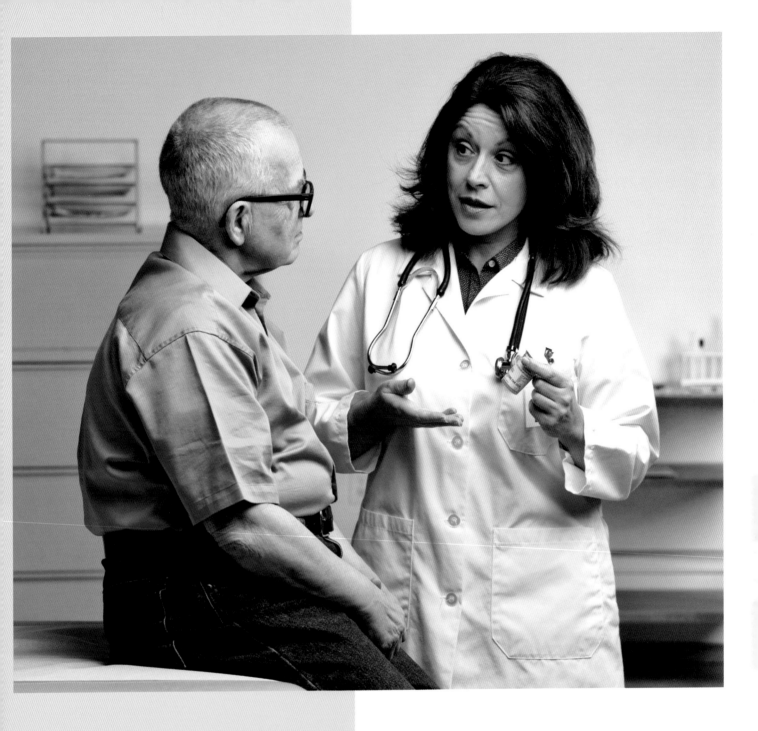

The doctor listens to our problems and prescribes medicines to cure our illnesses. We may need to visit the doctor more than once to get better.

A doctor who takes special care of children is called a paediatrician.

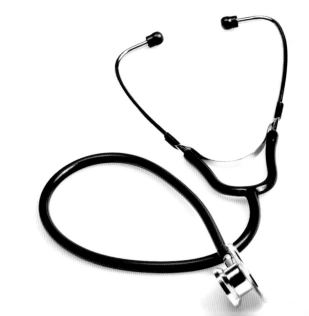

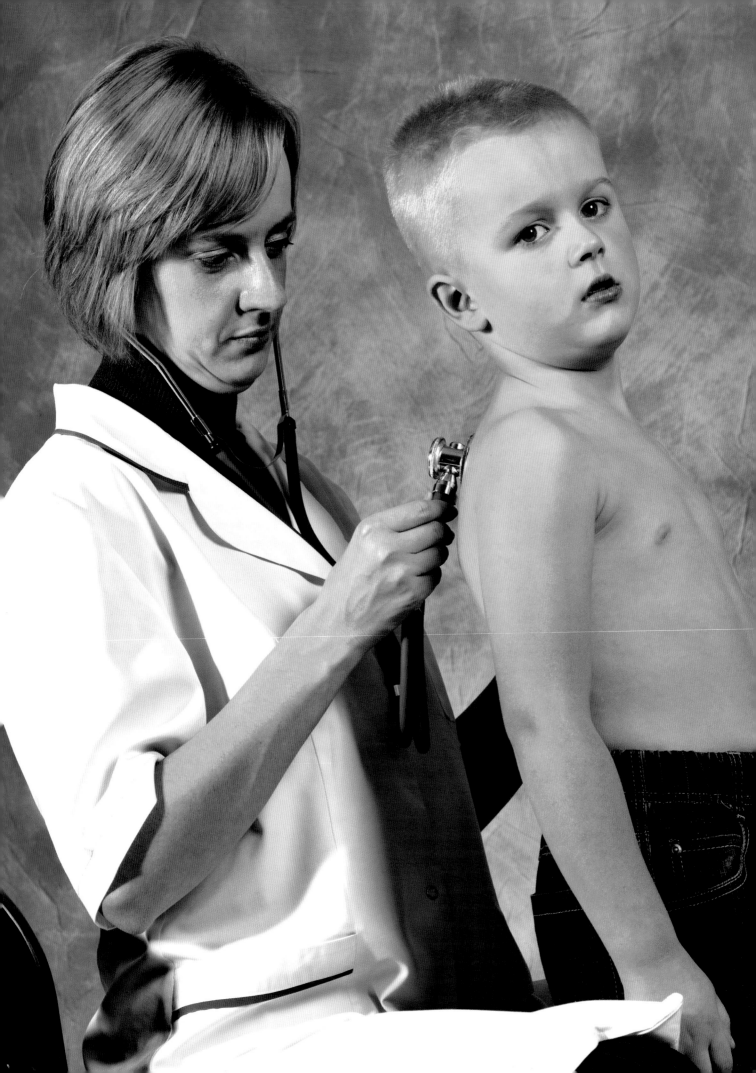

The doctor uses a stethoscope to listen to our heartbeat. That helps them to figure out what is wrong with us.

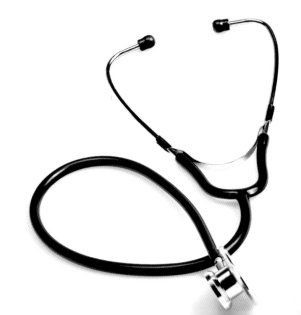

Doctors have all kinds of instruments to help them treat us. Some instruments can be used to look inside our body.

Nurses help doctors take care of patients. They are always around to look after the patient when the doctor is away.

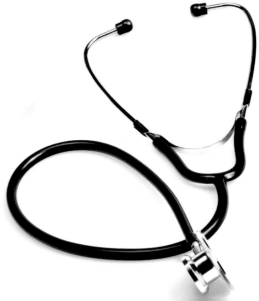

If something is wrong
with our throats,
the doctor asks us
to open our mouth
wide and say a loud
"aaaahhhhhh".

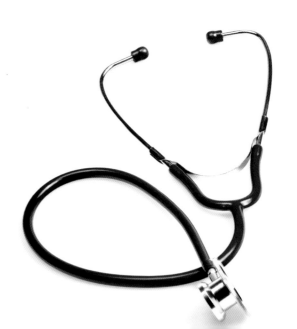

If we have a fever, the doctor can check our temperature with the help of a thermometer.

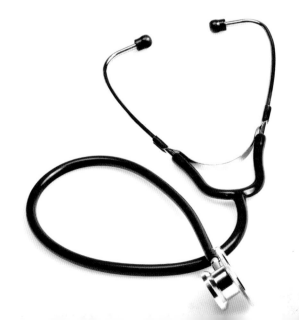

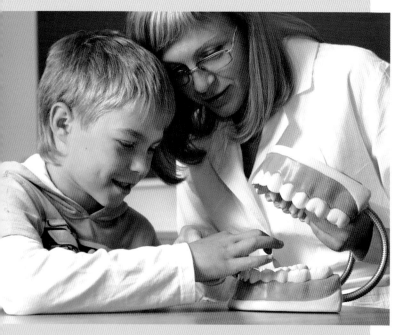

Dentists are doctors who take really good care of our teeth. They help us fight cavities, too.

Most of us are afraid to go to a dentist. But, if we want to keep our teeth and gums healthy, we have to visit the dentist regularly.

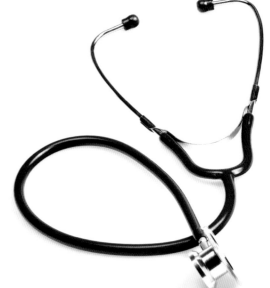

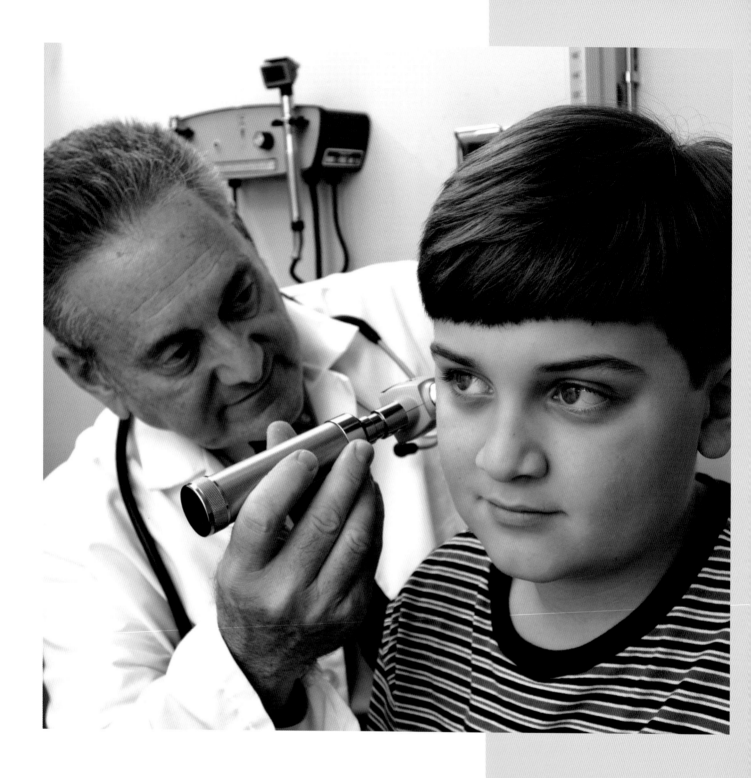

If we have an ear infection, we have to go to an ENT specialist for treatment. ENT stands for Ear, Nose and Throat.

An opthalmologist is the
doctor to go to if there
is something wrong with
our eyes. He can tell us
if we need spectacles or
contact lenses.

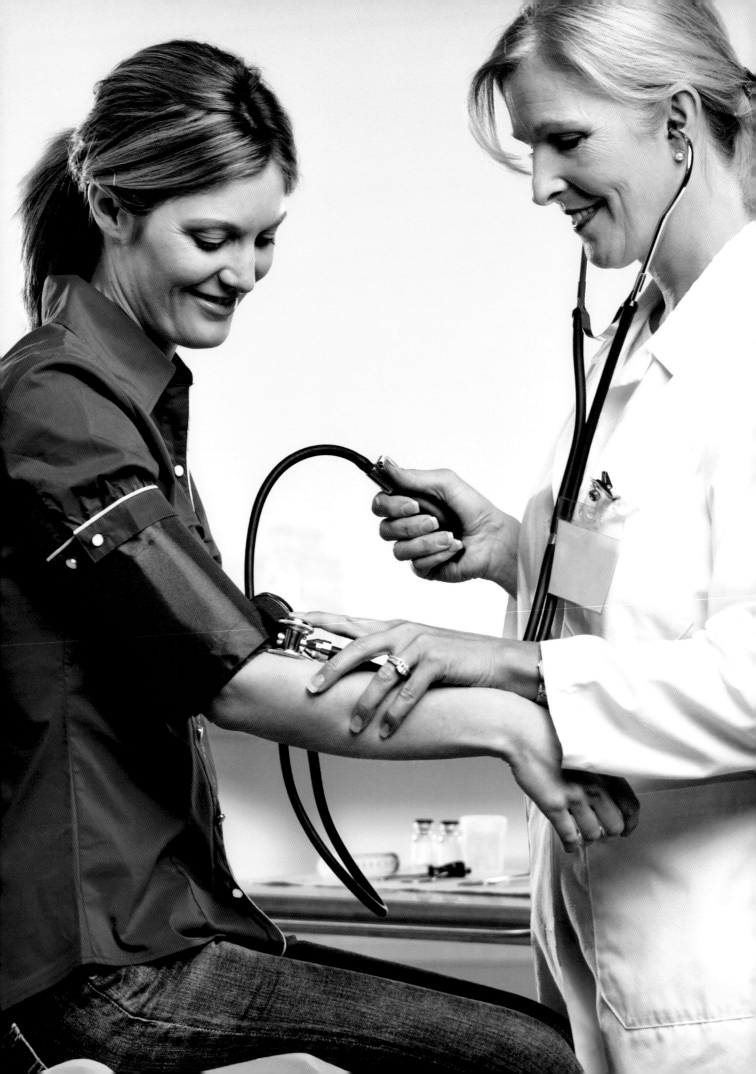

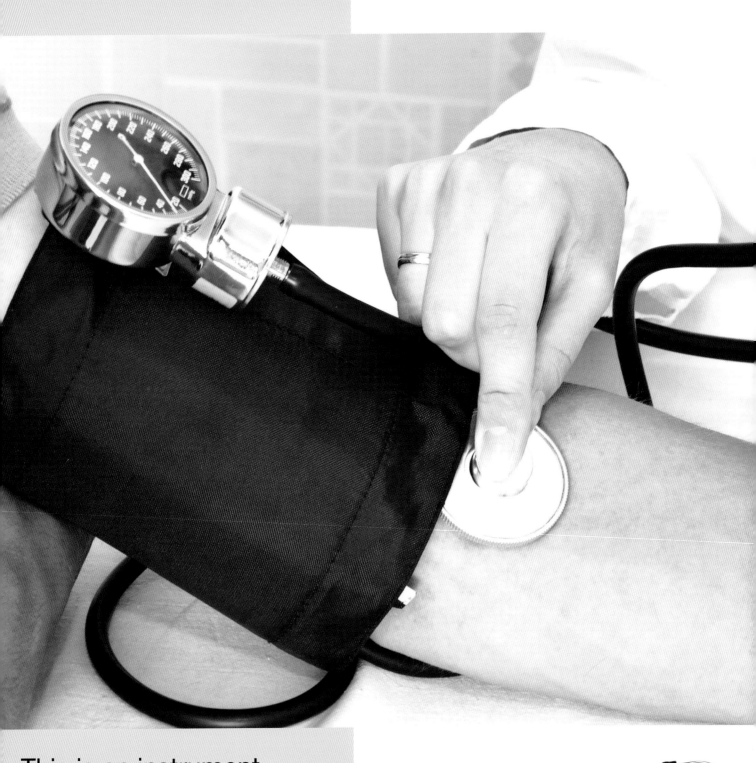

This is an instrument to measure our blood pressure. It is used with a stethoscope.
It has a very big name: sphygmomanometer.
Try and say it out loud!

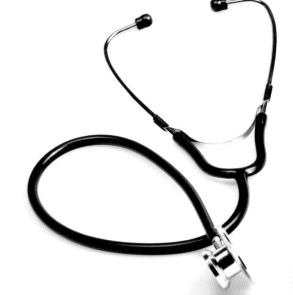

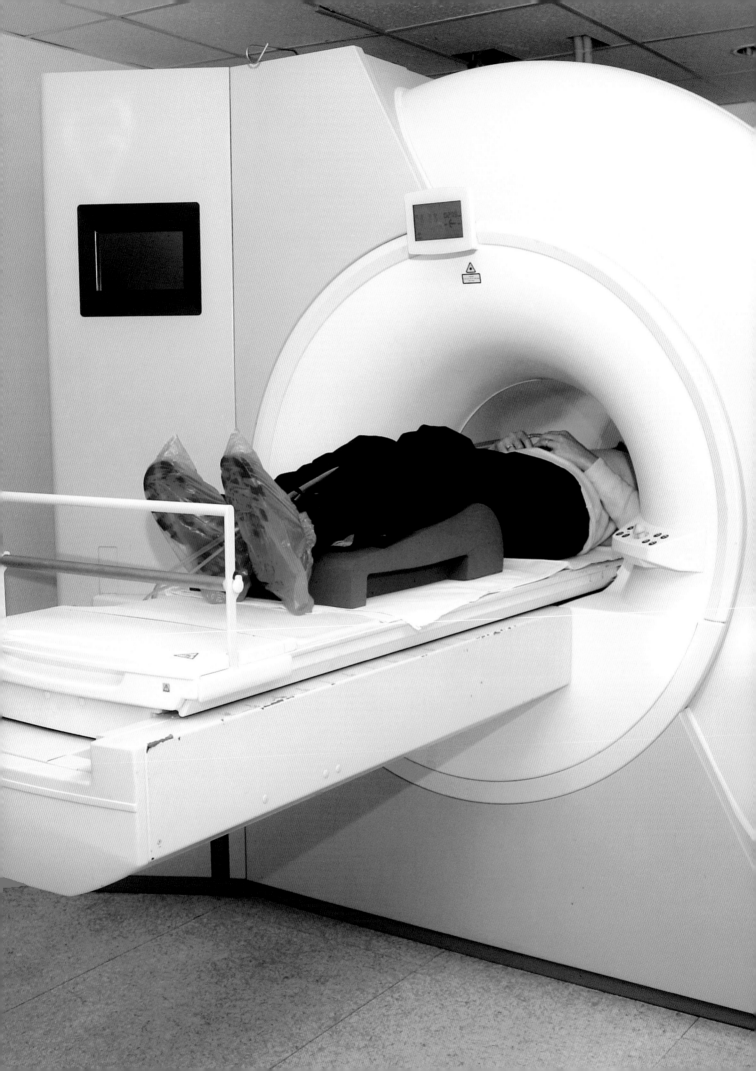

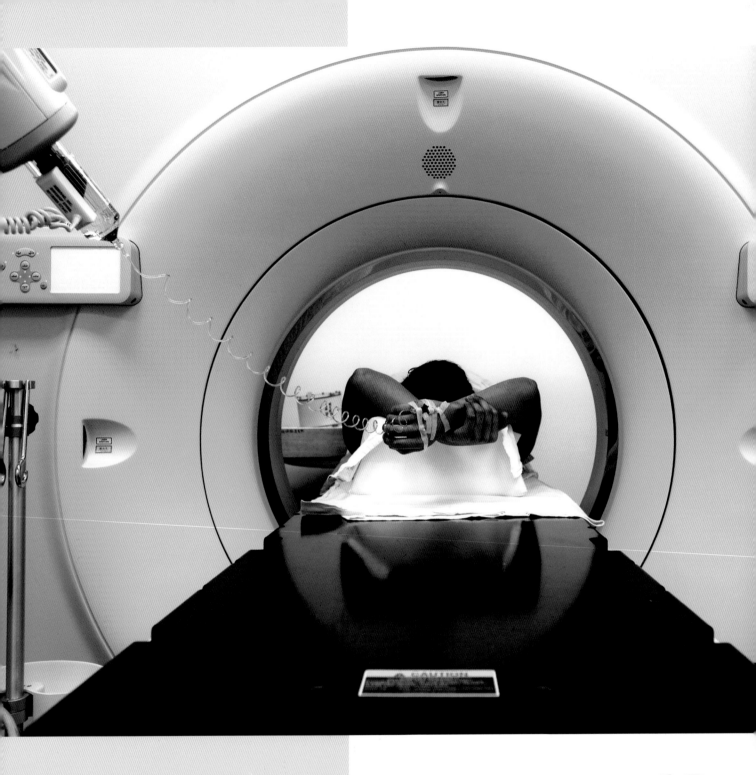

This is a machine that is used for MRIs. MRI stands for Magnetic Resonance Imaging. An MRI gives a detailed picture of the inside of our body.

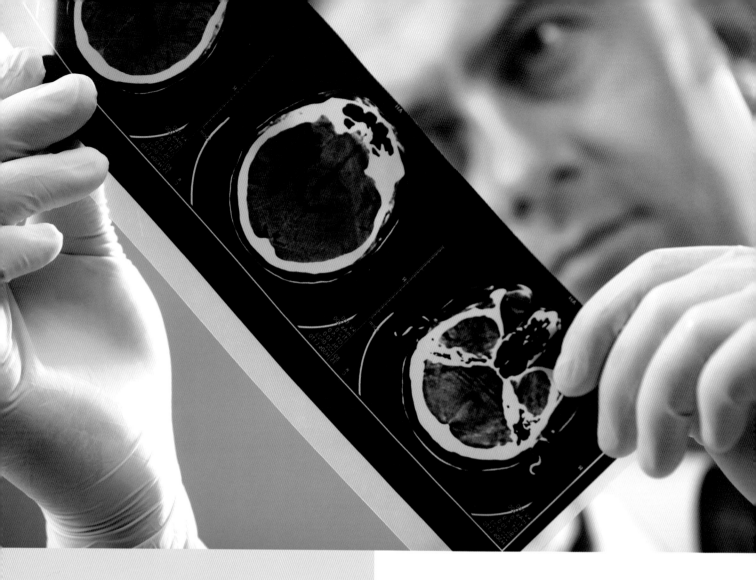

A CT scan is used
to check the inside
of our skull to see if
there are any injuries
or fractures.

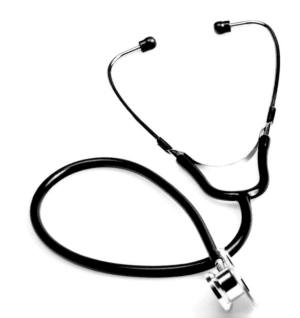

Doctors need to check X-ray reports to find out if we have fractured our bones. If there is a fracture, a plaster cast is normally used to fix it.

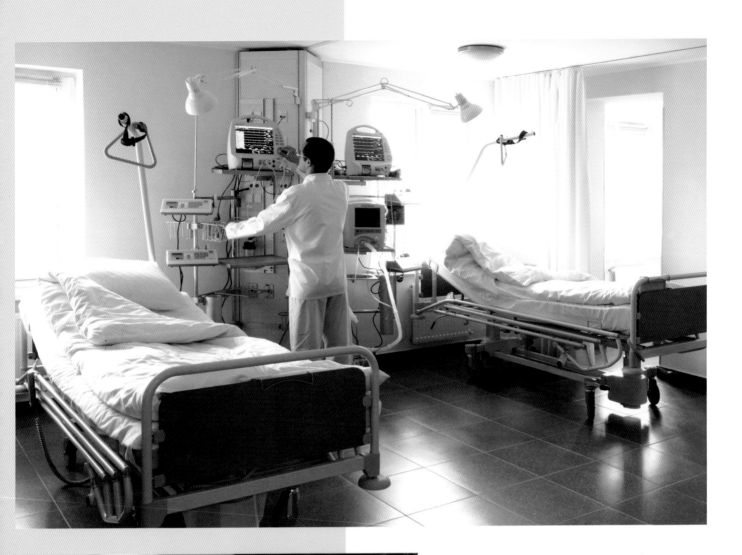

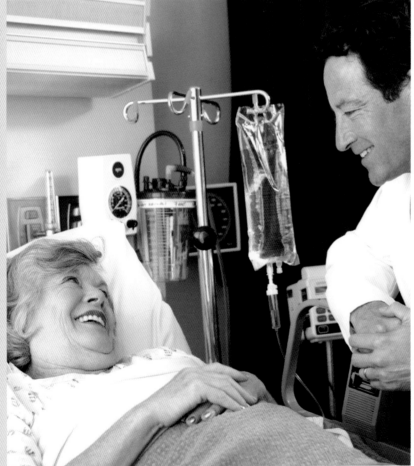

Most doctors work in hospitals. When people are very ill they have to be taken there to get better.

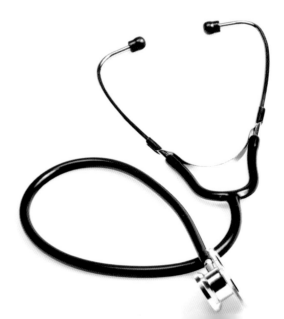

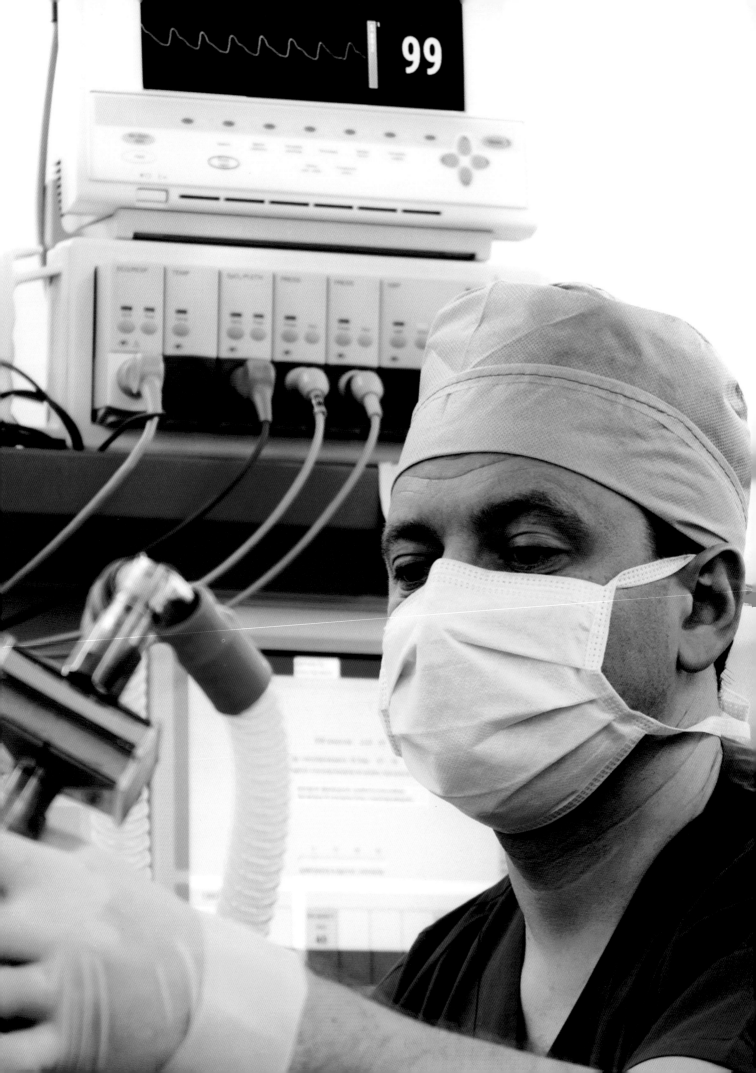

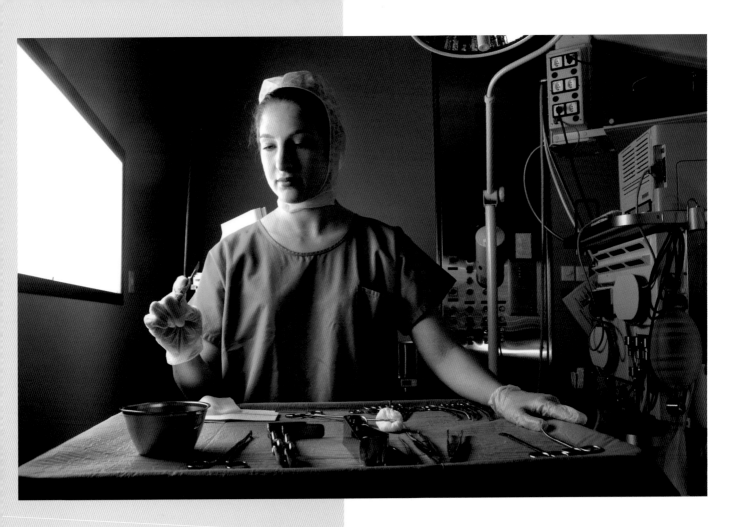

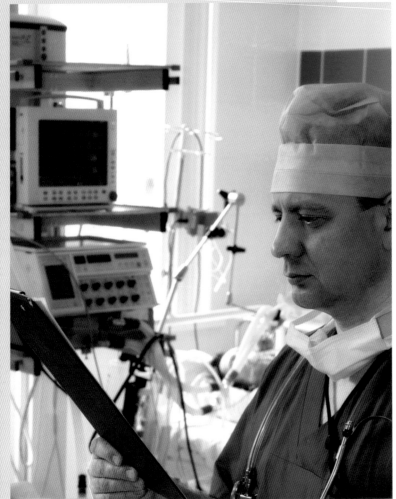

Sometimes doctors
need to perform surgery
to fix some problems.
The surgery may be
very complicated or
a minor and routine.

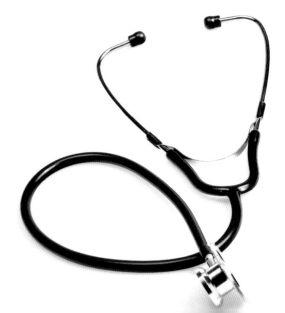

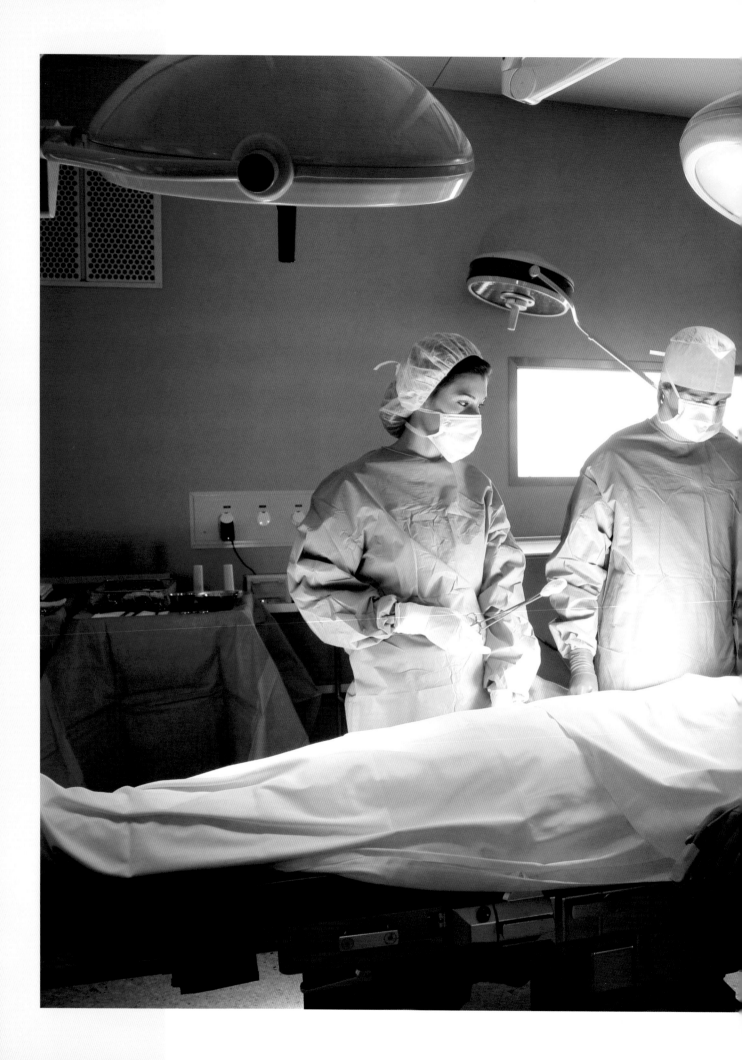

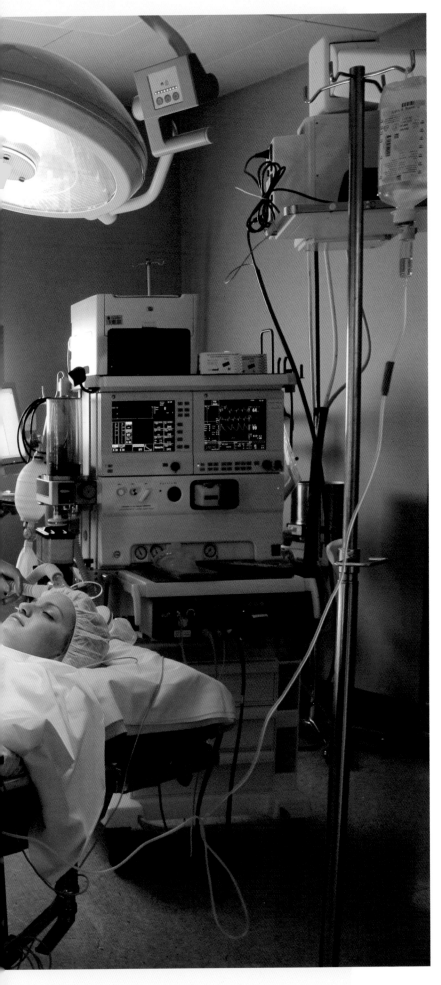

When surgeries have to be performed, doctors administer anaesthesia to prevent the patient from feeling any pain.

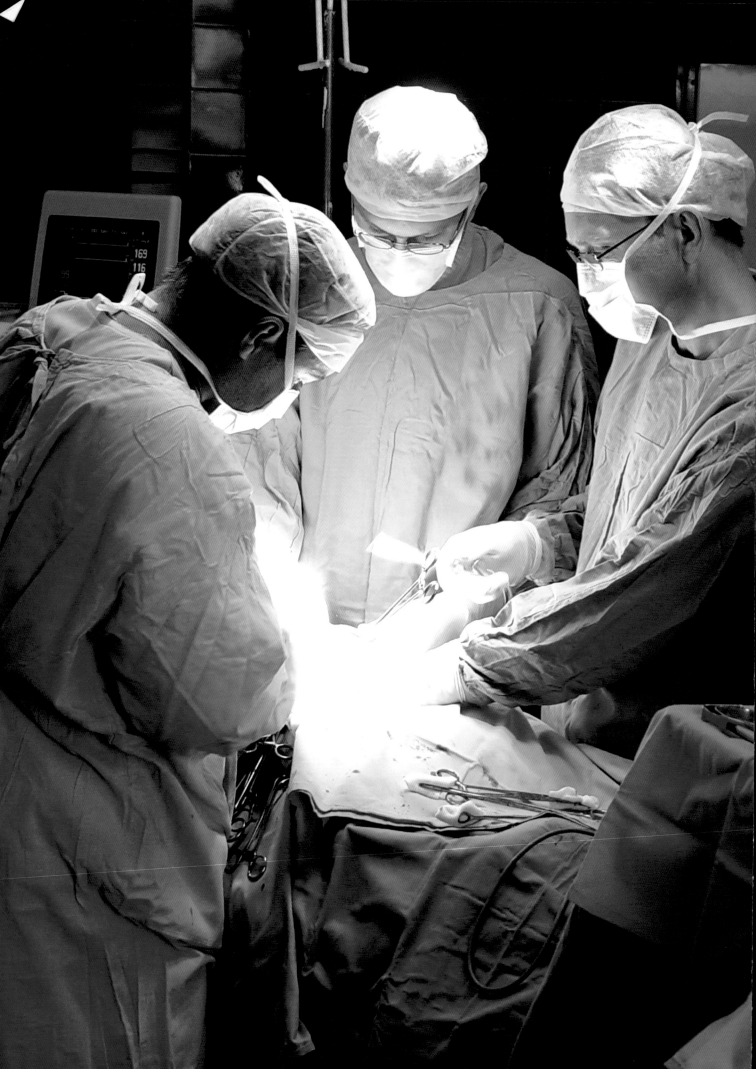

Major surgeries can take hours to perform. Several surgeons conduct these complicated procedures together where each surgeon does a specific job.

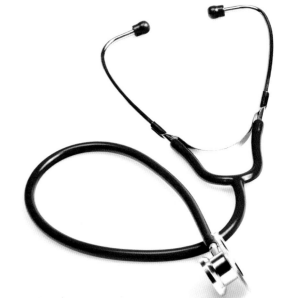

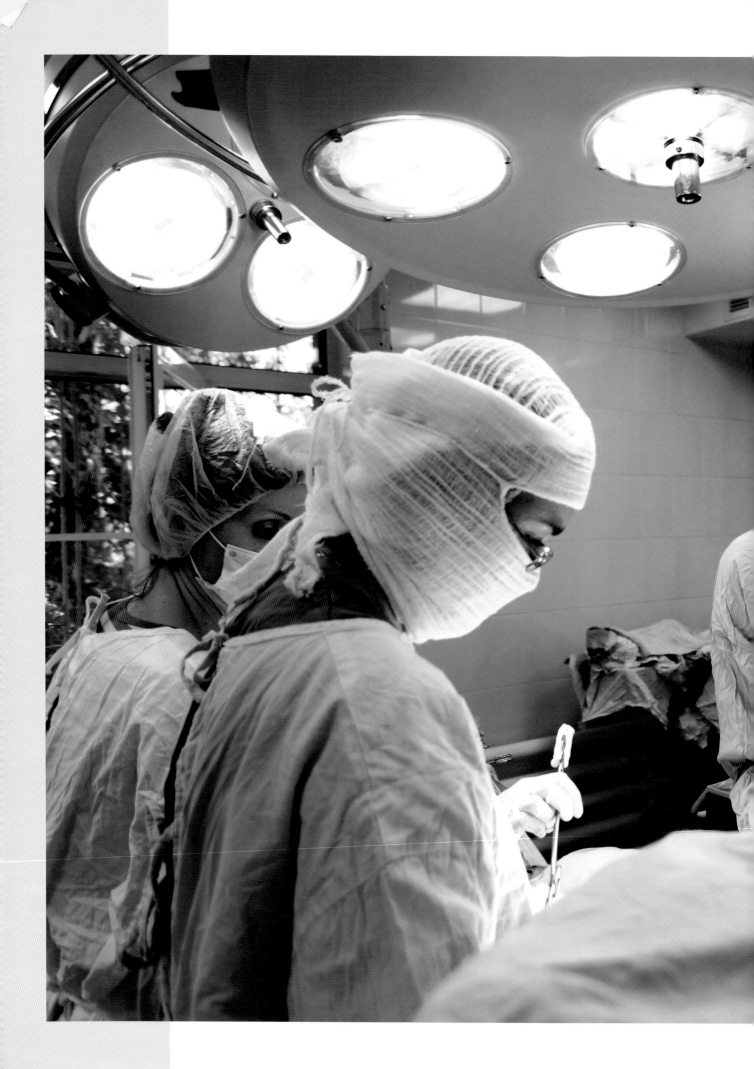

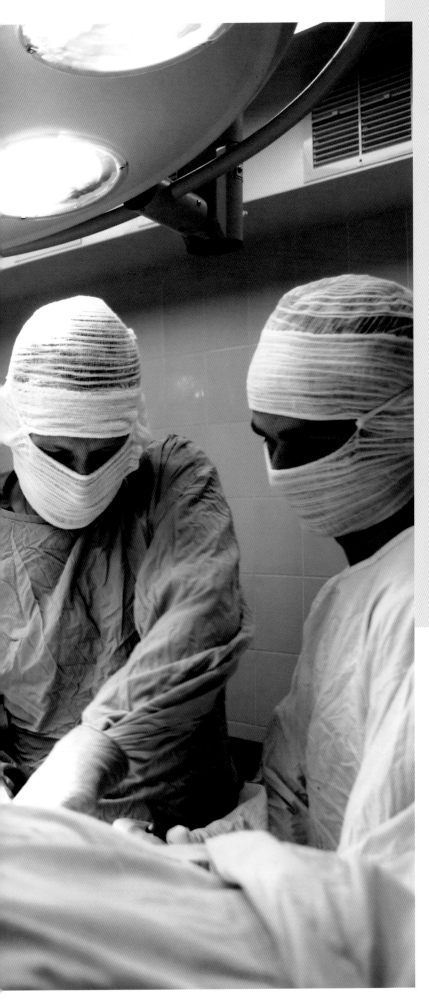

Before operating, surgeons clean themselves thoroughly and during the procedure they wear masks to prevent germs from getting into our blood.

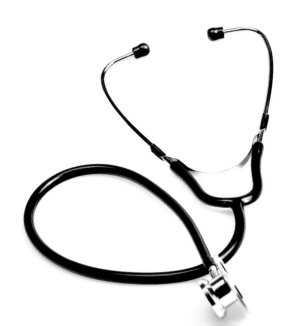

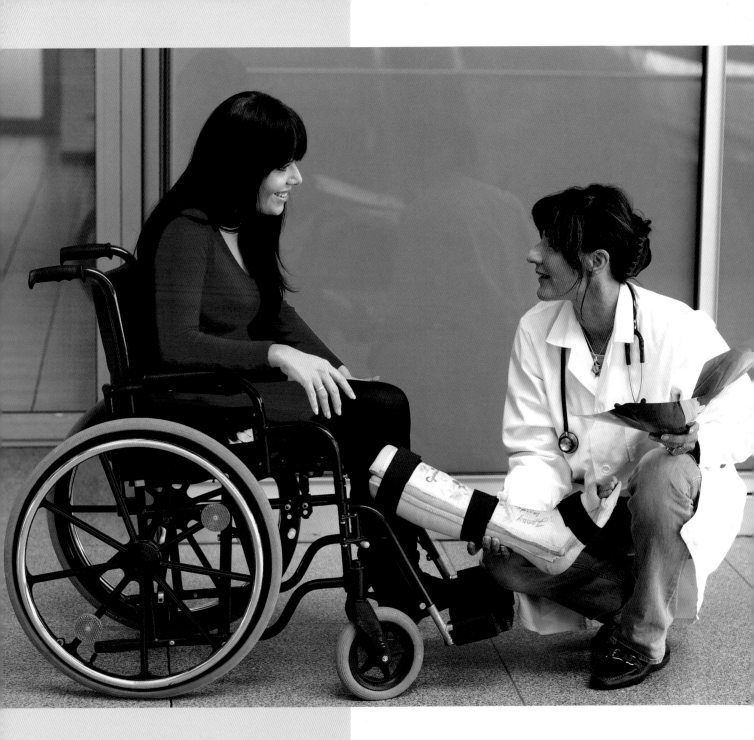

When one of our bones is broken, doctors use a plaster casing to heal the injury. Although it is painful, in most cases the bone heals completely.

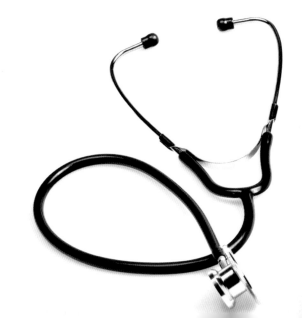

For more serious injuries different treatments are required. Sometimes metal plates and screws have to be inserted to hold bones in place.

Doctors usually prescribe medicines that come in the form of pills and syrups. These have to be taken in specific numbers or doses at particular times of the day.

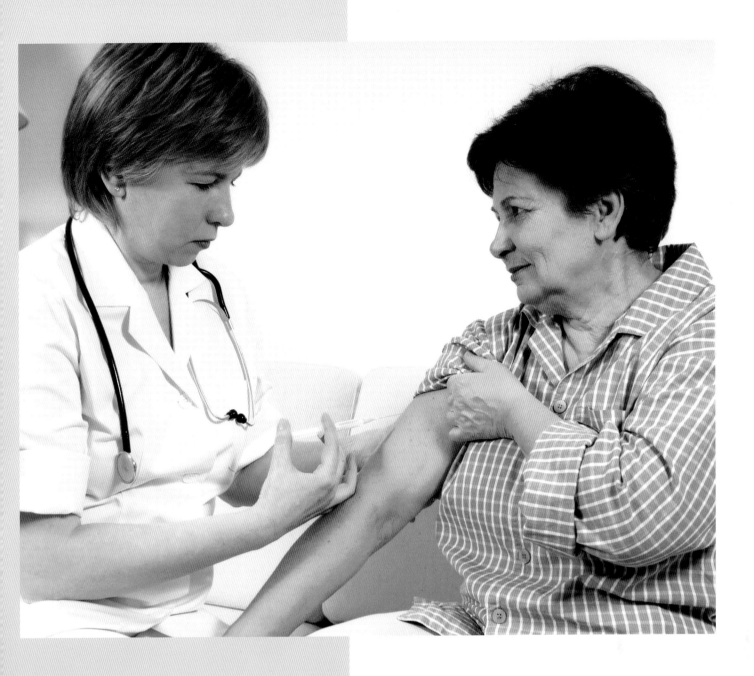

Sometimes though,
injections work better
than pills. Syringes
are used to push the
medicines into our body
with the help of needles.
It does not hurt too much.

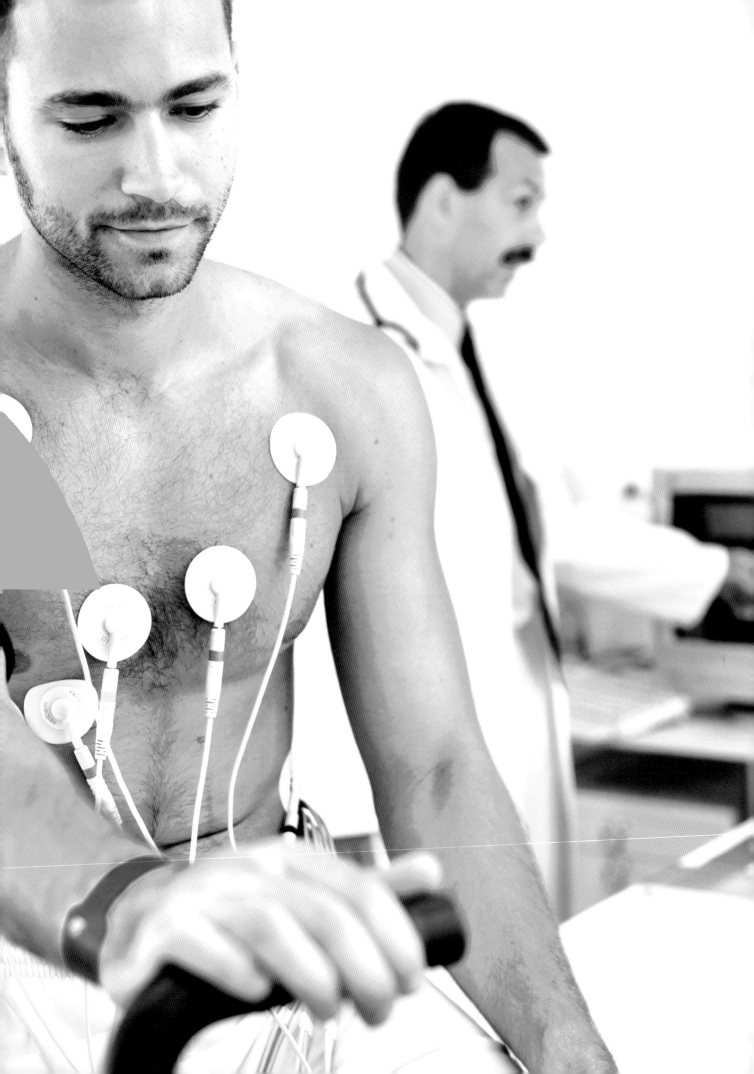

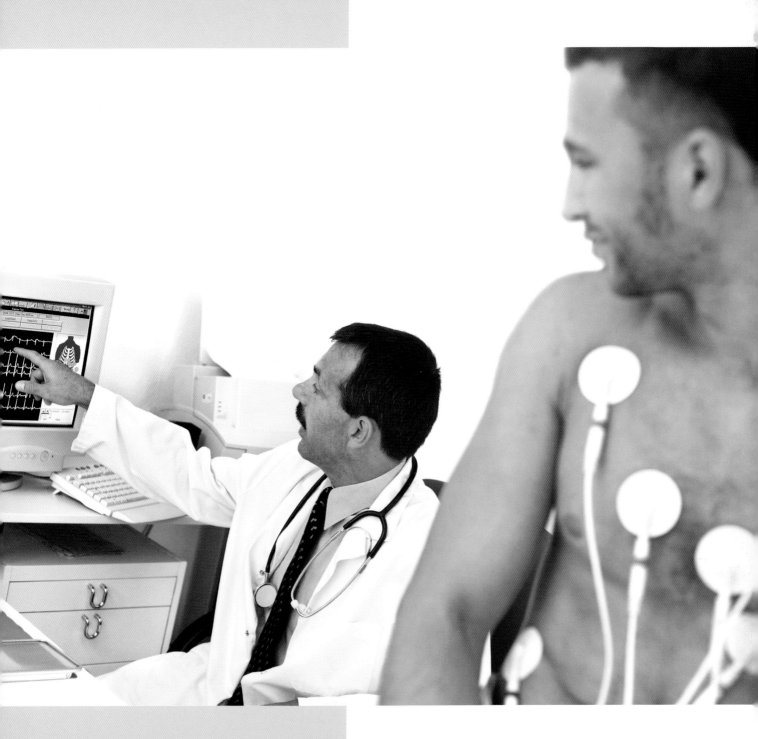

This is called
electrocardiography. It
is used to measure the
activity of the heart.
Those round patches
are skin electrodes.

In case of emergencies, patients are rushed to hospitals in ambulances. They might even be air-lifted to treatment centres.

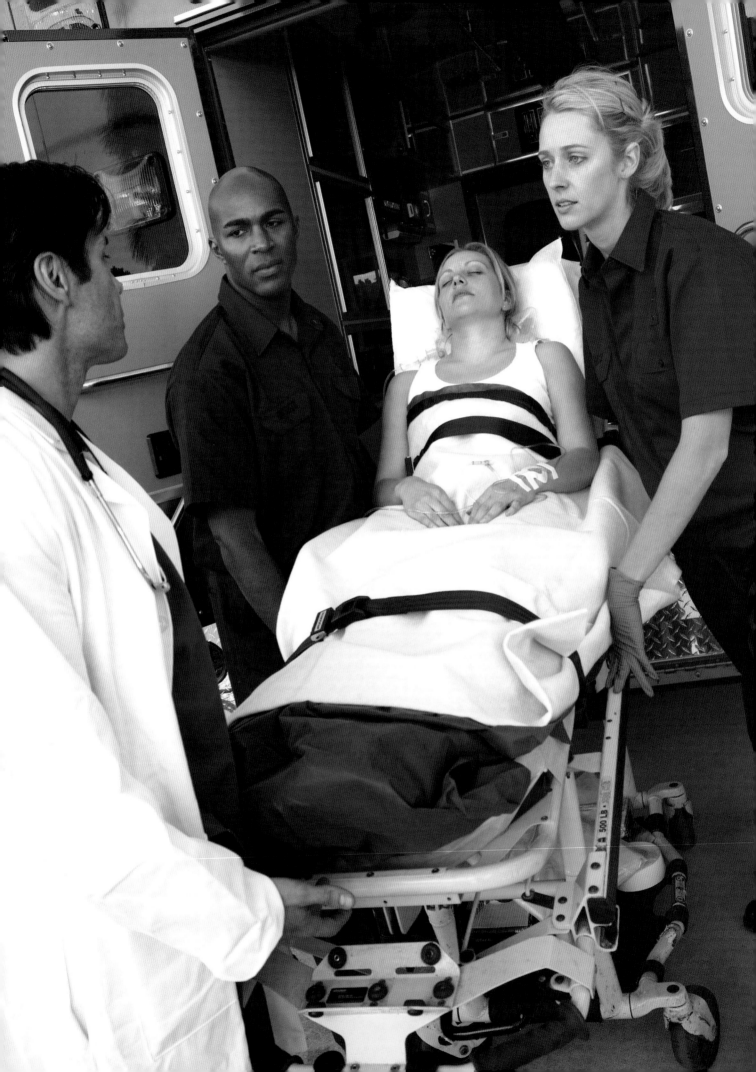

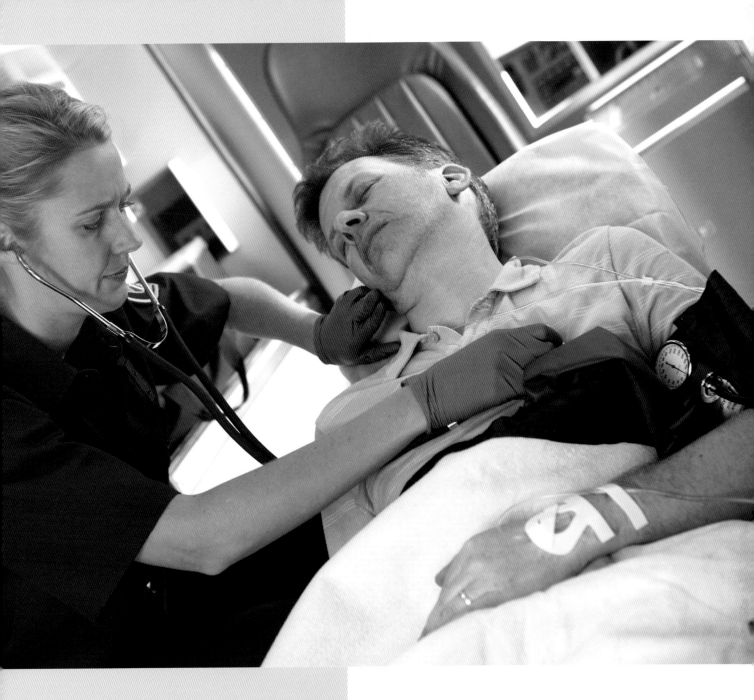

Doctors are trained to treat people in case of emergencies. There are special accident and emergency wards where people are taken for immediate treatment.

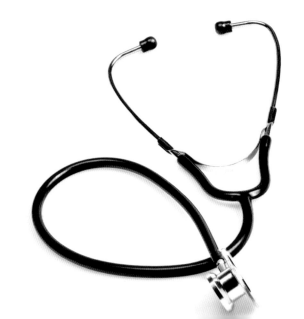

Veterinarians are doctors who treat animals. They look after your pets when they are not well. They also treat farm animals.

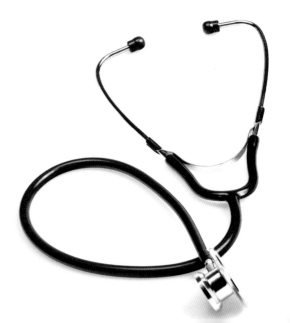

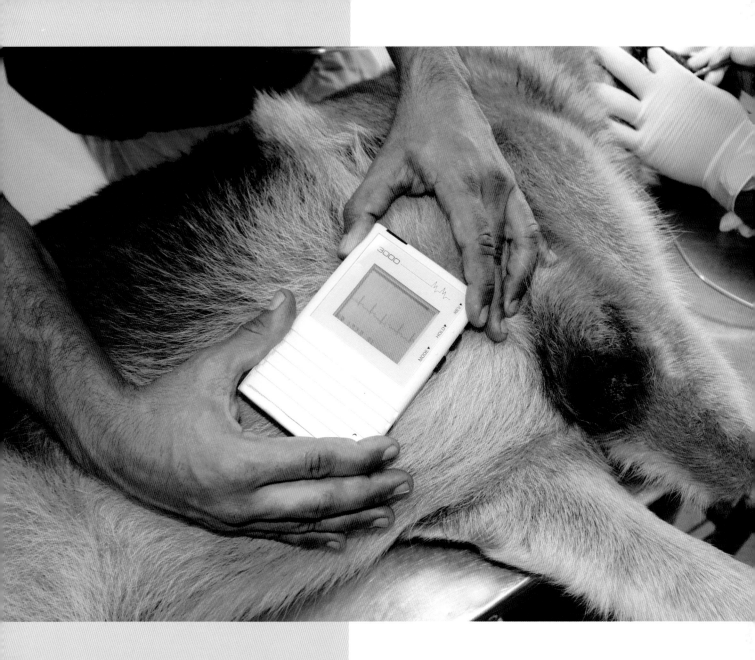

Vets can perform surgeries on animals if required. Like people, animals too can be given anaesthetics or could have their fractures plastered.

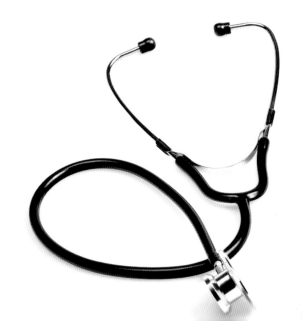

It takes a long time to become a doctor. A lot of serious studying has to be done. Before becoming doctors, students have to complete internships.

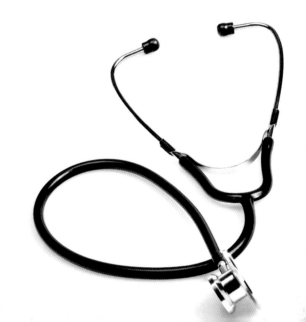

We have to trust our doctors to make us better. The doctors, in turn, try their best to help us get back to our normal lives.

GLOSSARY

Anaesthetic:	a drug to induce the loss of feeling
Cavity:	hollow space or pit in a tooth
Contaminate:	to make something impure
CT scan:	an image of the inside of the body using x-rays
Doctor:	a person who is trained to treat illnesses and injuries
Fracture:	a break in a bone
Heal:	to make healthy
Inject:	force medicine into the body
Instruments:	tools and equipment used by doctors
Internship:	working as a trainee in a job to gain experience

Prescribe: give medicines

Procedure: steps taken to conduct surgery

Specialist: a doctor trained to treat a specific part of the body

Sphygmomanometer: an instrument used to measure the blood pressure

Stethoscope: an instrument used to listen to the sounds inside the body

Surgery: treating a person manually using instruments

Thermometer: an instrument used to measure the temperature of a person

Treat: relieve or cure an ailment or disease

Veterinarian : an animal doctor